Piano Technic

Book 3

Frances Clark ® *Library for Piano Students*

" Technic lives in the brain of the pianist . "
— Busoni

Studies by Marion McArtor

Selected and correlated by Frances Clark

Edited by Louise Goss

Summy-Birchard Inc.

exclusively distributed by
Warner Bros. Publications Inc.
265 Secaucus Road
Secaucus, New Jersey 07096-2037

PREFACE

The six volumes of the PIANO TECHNIC series are designed as technical preparation for the piano literature which the student plays at each of the corresponding levels.

Of course, no book can teach technic. But a book *can* organize the presentation of technic into a logical and concise order of development.

As you study the table of contents you will see that the organization is in chapters, each chapter devoted to one of the basic positions which the hand takes as it plays any piece of music.

As you study the etudes themselves you will see that:

1. Every etude rehearses a specific technical point.

2. The technical point occurs over and over throughout the piece.

3. There is always as much experience for the left hand as for the right hand.

4. There is equal experience for all ten fingers.

5. The technical practice is done in a musical context, not in finger exercises.

Our aim is to provide musical situations so appealing that they will encourage the student to do concentrated and repeated technical practice. This is the purpose of the PIANO TECHNIC series.

FRANCES CLARK

TABLE OF CONTENTS
(Based on Positions of the Hand)

I. *Five-finger position*

II. *Extensions*
(combined with five-finger positions)

III. *Contractions*

IV. *Diatonic crossings (scales)*

V. *Interval crossings (arpeggios)*

A. Crossing over the thumb

B. Sliding the thumb under

C. Crossings over and under

VI. *Miscellaneous*

A. Sustained and moving voices in one hand

B. Trills

C. Rhythmic study: Two notes against three

D. Repeated notes

E. Glissandos

F. Accompaniment figures

I. Five-finger position

Allegro moderato (♩= about 116)

1a.

Allegro moderato (♩= about 116)

1b.

Allegretto ($\quarternote$ = about 96)

2.

6

Allegretto (♩ = about 108)

3.

7

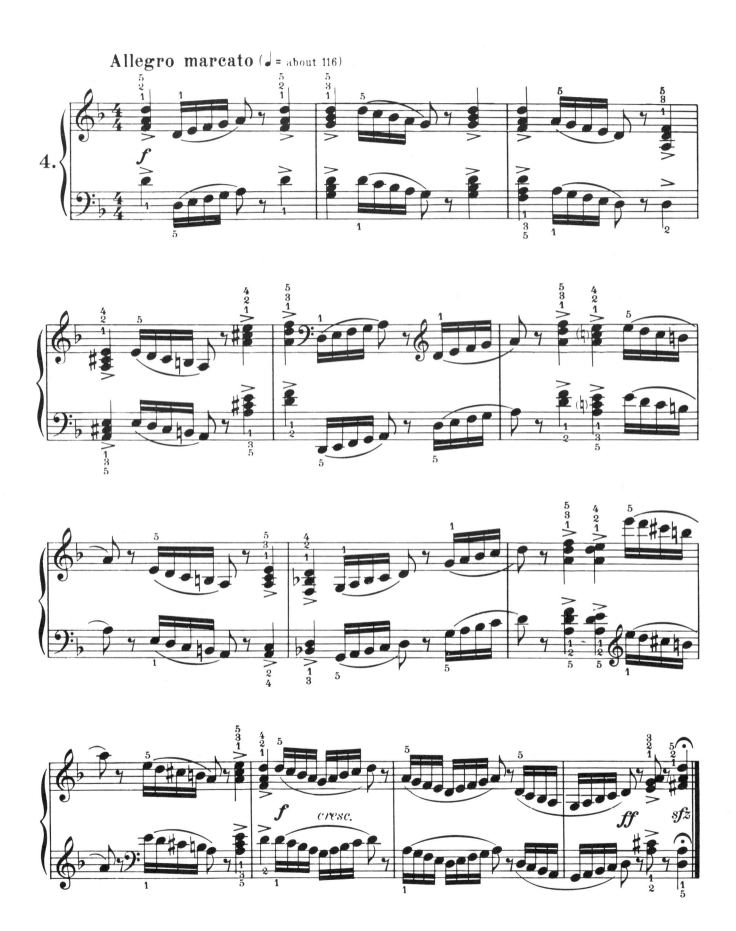

evenness btn. the hands
we do technic by listening

II. *Extensions (combined with five-finger positions)*

Moderato con moto ($\quad$ = about 88)
sempre legato

8.

12

Allegro con spirito (♩ = about 120)

9.

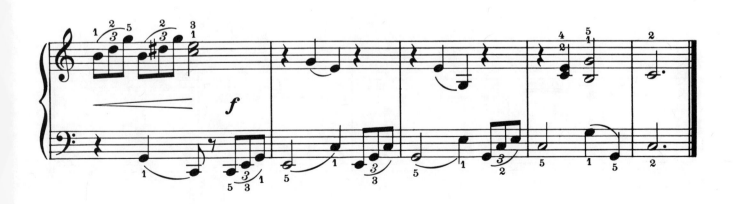

13

10a.

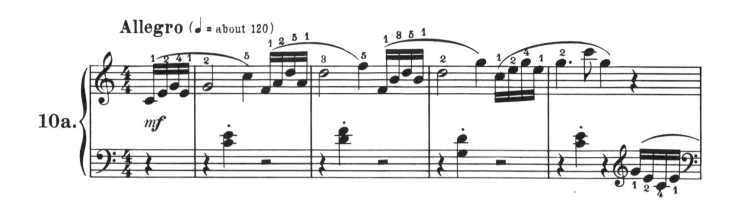

10b.

Allegro (♩ = about 112)

11a.

Allegro moderato (♩ = about 112)

11b.

15

Moderato (♩ = about 100)

12.

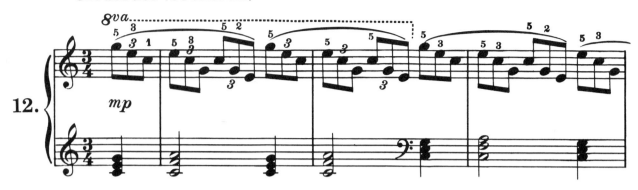

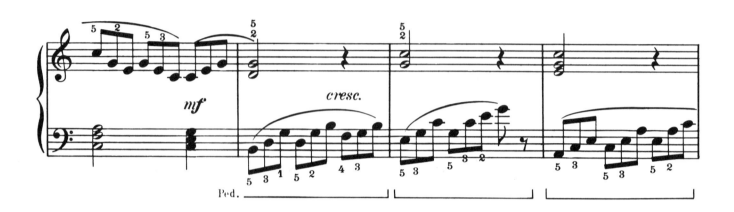

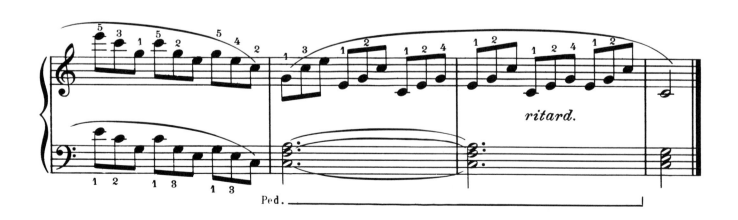

Vivace (♩ = about 120)

13.

Allegro (♩ = about 132)

III. *Contractions*

IV. *Diatonic crossings (scales)*

Moderato con moto (♩ = about 80)

19.

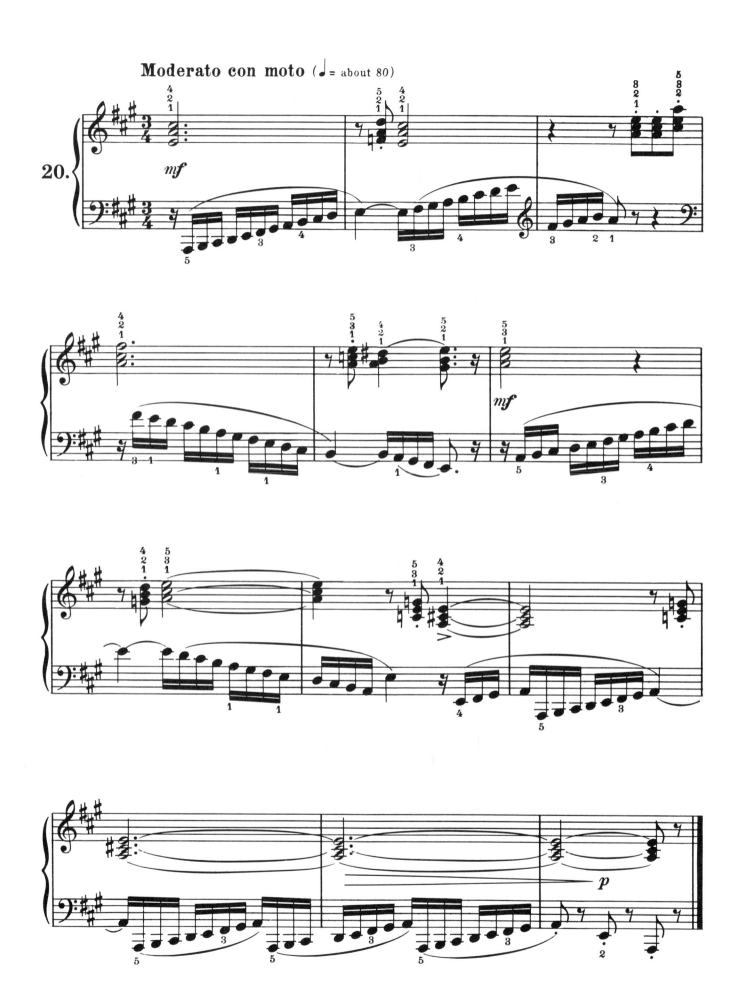

Moderato con moto (♩ = about 80)

20.

Moderato con moto (♩ = about 80)

21.

V. *Interval crossings (arpeggios)*

23a.

23b.

VI. *Miscellaneous*

A. Sustained and moving voices in one hand

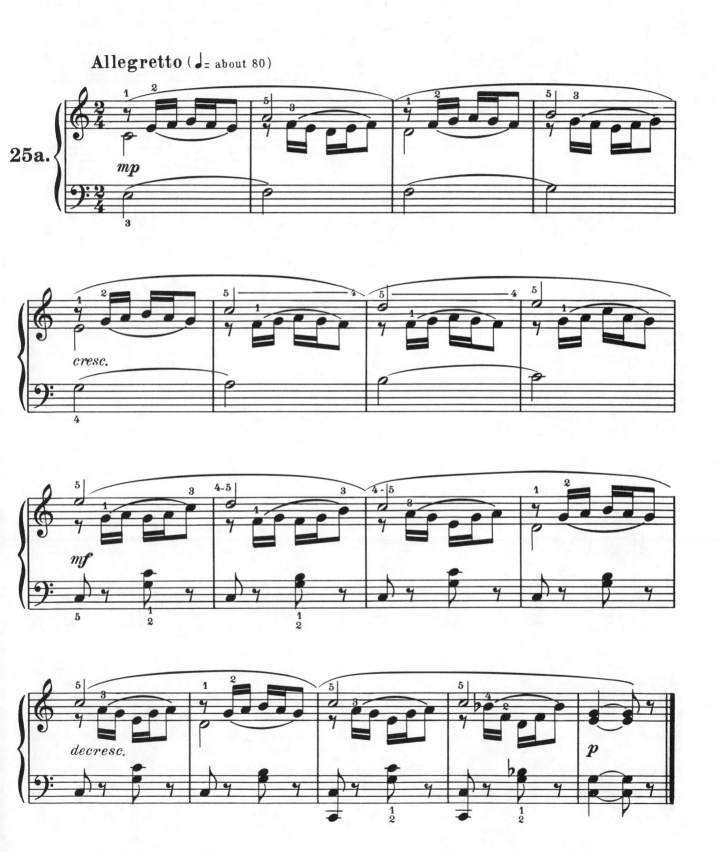

B. Trills

Slowly (♩ = about 88)

27.

C. Rhythmic study: Two notes against three

30.

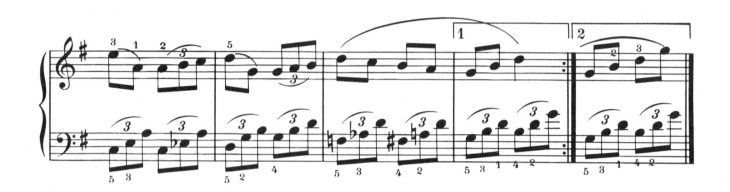

D. Repeated notes

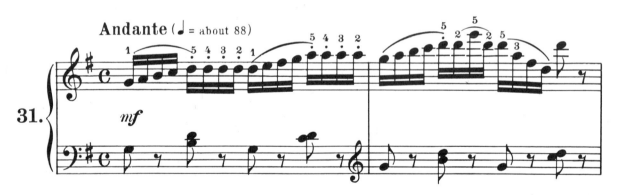

31.

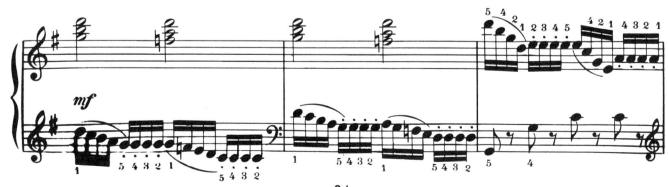

34

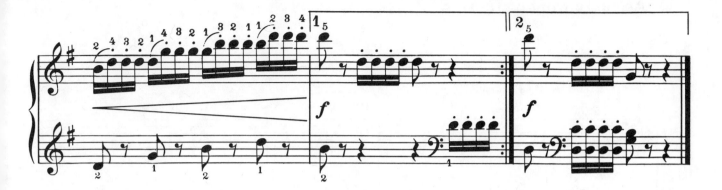

E. Glissandos

F. Accompaniment figures

33.

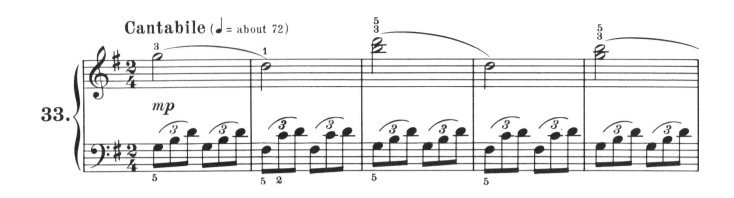

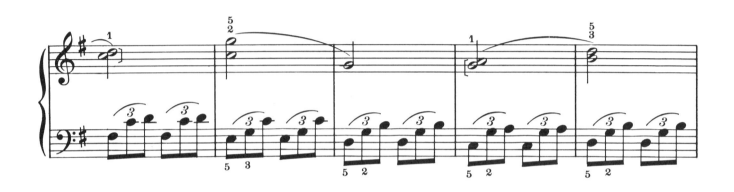

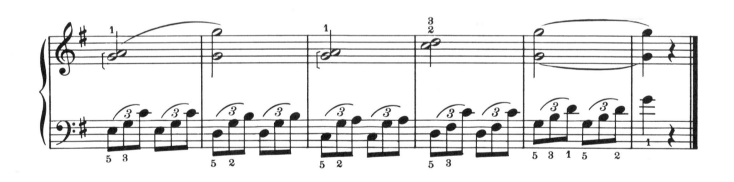

34.

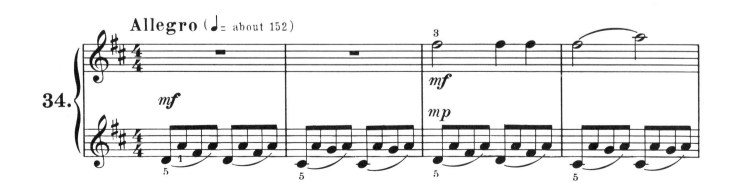

Vivace (♩ = about 152)

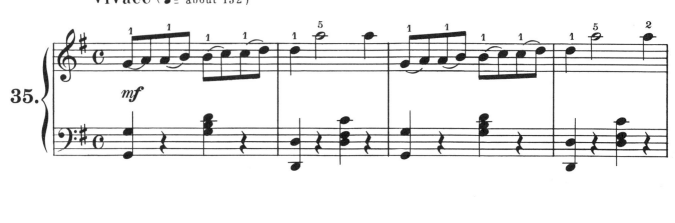

35.

Vivo (♩ = about 152)